by Jennifer Brozek

Other Books by Jennifer Brozek

Anthologies

Grants Pass – Morrigan Books
Close Encounters of the Urban Kind – Apex Publications
Beauty Has Her Way – Dark Quest Books
Human Tales – Dark Quest Books
Beast Within 2: Predator & Prey – Graveside Tales
Space Tramps – Flying Pen Press
Human for a Day – DAW
Beast Within 3: Oceans Unleashed – Graveside Tales*

Fiction

In a Gilded Light – Dark Quest Books
The Lady of Seeking in the City of Waiting – Dark Quest Books

Non-Fiction

The Little Finance Book That Could – Shaker Books

Role Playing Books

Players Guide to Castlemourn (with Ed Greenwood) – Margaret Weis Productions
Proverbial Monsters – White Wolf
The Ross-Allen Letters (with Dylan Birtolo) – Rogue Games
Shanghai Vampocalypse – Savage Mojo
Millennium Knights – Savage Mojo*
Colonial Gothic: Locations – Rogue Games*

* = Forthcoming

Industry Talk: An Insider's Look at Writing RPGs and Editing Anthologies

Jennifer Brozek

Apocalypse Ink Productions
Kenmore, Washington

Credits

PUBLISHED BY

Apocalypse Ink Productions
6830 NE Bothell Way, STE C #404
Kenmore, WA 98028
http://www.apocalypse-ink.com/

Based on previously published columns by
Jennifer Brozek: *Dice & Deadlines* and *The
Making of an Anthology*.

Interior art and design by Jeff Brozek

ISBN: 978-0-9855323-1-4

Praise for *Industry Talk*

"Want to write for games? Want to navigate the dark labyrinths and endless mazes of freelancing? Let Brozek be your guide."
– Chuck Wendig, game designer and author of *500 Ways to be a Better Writer*

"If you're going to make that leap, though, and come over to the freelance side to join us, don't go blind. Do your research. Ask questions. Read this book."
– Matt Forbeck, game designer and author of *Amortals* and *Vegas Knights*

"To those looking to save hours of field research into two highly specialized and hard-to-crack fields, Jennifer Brozek's pragmatic, down-to-earth advice serves as an essential clue-dispenser."
– Robin D. Laws, game designer and author of *Hamlet's Hit Points*

"*Industry Talk* collects some of the best, most practical advice I've ever read for game-writing and anthology-editing freelancers. It covers the most challenging aspects of what freelancing is like and offers useful, no-nonsense strategies to help you get started and keep the work coming in. Freelancing isn't for everyone, but this book contains the information you need to make it, if you're willing to put in the effort and live with the risk.

Brozek tackles the challenges inherent in freelance RPG writing and anthology editing with practicality and a matter-of-fact tone. She pulls no punches about the pitfalls of the job. While game-writing is a dream job for many people, it is no cake-walk.

As Brozek says, "Freelancing for the RPG author is an active thing. You need to look for (or make) the opportunities and grab them." The first opportunity you should grab is this book. It will give you the information you need to decide whether you're dedicated enough to become a freelance RPG writer or anthology editor, and if you decide you are, then it will tell you how to go about it. Take Brozek's advice to heart. She knows what she's talking about."
– Angel Leigh McCoy, writer for *Guild Wars 2* and editor of *Wily Writers Podcast*

Dedicated to Jeff.
Thank you for helping make the industry happen.

Acknowledgements

Putting together a book like this is a group effort and there are many people to thank for that effort.

Thank you to those people who invited me to write for them: E. Foley of Geek's Dream Girl, Emily Care Boss of RPGirl Zine, and Jason Sizemore of Apex Publications. Without them, this book would not exist.

Thank you to those people who worked on this book with me: Ivan Ewert for the many iterations of the cover until we got it just right, Matt Forbeck for an excellent foreword, and to Lily Cohen-Moore for your editing expertise.

Finally, thank you to my husband, Jeff. You are the keystone that keeps everything together.

Table of Contents

Industry Talk: Foreword by Matt Forbeck

I've been a freelance writer and game designer for over twenty years now, and I love it. It offers me the chance to work on all sorts of different projects, to create fun things, and to entertain (and sometimes even inform) others for a living. What more could I ask?

Well, other than being paid ridiculous sums of cash?

It's possible to make a decent living as a freelancer, but it's not easy. For many, the worst part is figuring out how to break in, but it can be just as tricky to know what you're supposed to do once you're in. After all, you're working for yourself, and that kind of job doesn't come with an employee manual that spells out what you need to do and outlines the kinds of pitfalls you should watch out for.

In this book, though, Jennifer Brozek gives you the next best thing: the details on how she got started and how she treats her freelancing business as just that, a business. Then she goes on to bore down into a particular type of freelancing—that of the anthology editor—and unearths the details about it to show you just how it really works.

Freelancing isn't for everyone. It takes a strong gut to be able to go out on your own and make your living by your own wits alone. Most people prefer the comforts that come with having a steady job: a regular paycheck (so you can budget for the future), division of labor (so you can concentrate on what you do best), and a full slate of benefits (including items many consider indispensable, like a pension and health insurance).

I've rarely been swayed by such things myself. I'm fortunate enough to have started out at it when I was young and could play the starving artist for a few years without anyone noticing much of a difference between my state then and when I was in college. I also married young and qualify for health-care benefits through my wife, who has a Masters in Social Work.

And how many people have you heard of working as freelance social workers?

Still, the biggest reason many people stick with a full-time job rather than take the plunge into freelancing is that they prefer the security that's supposed to come with such things. If you're working as a teacher or on the assembly line at General Motors, it often seems like you're insulated from the wild vagaries that afflict the freelancer's checking account.

You don't have to look far, though, to see how wrongheaded that idea can be, especially in turbulent economic times, during which no one's job seems safe. No one can fire you from being a freelancer.

Sure, work can dry up, forcing you to explore other avenues. Clients can be frustrating to handle and may even try to stiff you. And you may find that you're not raking in nearly as much as you think you're worth.

But you get to be your own boss. You get to make the big decisions and call all your own shots. Rather than rely on someone else to keep at bay the wolf at the door, you get to do it yourself. In the end, succeed or fail, the only one who gets the legitimate credit or blame for it is you.

To me, that offers more security than a traditional job. As a freelancer, I don't have to worry about my company making its quarterly numbers. I never have to fear that my boss will threaten to fire me if I take off time to take my kids to the doctor or to see them in a game or a play. When Christmas comes around, I don't fret that someone above me might be tempted to cut my salary as a temporary way of improving the company's year-end accounts.

Sure, I have to work for several clients at once, but that spreads around the risk that any one of them might fold up or implode on me through no fault of my own. That's the secret of any wise investor who wants to succeed over the long term: to spread the risk around. And what investment means more to you than your career?

If you're going to make that leap, though, and come over to the freelance side to join us, don't go blind. Do your research. Ask questions. Figure out what you need to know.

Read this book.

But don't just take Jennifer's advice. It's a good model for what to do and how to behave, but like all models, it's not the real thing. Once you're done with this book, find others.

Better yet, find the people who do what you want to do for a living, and ask them about it. Most of us are happy to share our hard-won knowledge with others, if only for the simple satisfaction that the lessons learned from those painful knocks might do some good for others outside of just ourselves.

In the end, of course, you need to step up and make your own decisions. You need to learn to rely on yourself and to put aside any excuses that let you off the hook. That's when you'll have what it takes to become successful as a freelancer — or at anything else you care to do.

Good luck!

Matt Forbeck has been a full-time creator of award-winning games and fiction since 1989. He has designed collectible card games, roleplaying games, miniatures games, board games, and toys, and has written novels, short fiction, comic books, motion comics, nonfiction, essays, and computer game scripts and stories for a slew of clients. He has sixteen novels published to date, including the award-nominated Guild Wars: Ghosts of Ascalon *and the critically acclaimed* Amortals *and* Vegas Knights. *His latest work includes the* Magic: The Gathering *comic book and the historical horror novel* Carpathia. *He is currently in the middle of his 12 for '12 project, in which he's using Kickstarter to help fund writing a novel every month this year. For more about him and his work, visit Forbeck.com.*

ROLE-PLAYING GAMES

Dice & Deadlines

When I was contracted by Geek's Dream Girl to write *Dice & Deadlines*, I was only sure of what I wanted to write for the first half of the year. However, the more I wrote about what it was like to write in the RPG industry, the more I found I had to say; cautionary stories, advice, and things I wish I had known when I first started.

By the time I was done, I was grateful to E. Foley and Geek's Dream Girl for giving me the opportunity to say what I wanted to say. To put the column in context, I asked E. Foley to talk about the website that gave my column a home.

Geek's Dream Girl by E. Foley

GeeksDreamGirl.com is a labor of geek love with geek girl E. Foley at the helm. E wanted to have a place on the web where she could write about geeky topics and use her writing skills to help single geeks find love. The site has grown a lot since then, but the core mission is the same – to help geeks find each other.

On the site, you'll find articles about dating, online dating, and relationships (with a geek bent); Dungeons & Dragons, Pathfinder, and other RPGs and LARPs; working in geeky industries; anime, manga, and otaku; comic books, graphic novels, and webcomics; video games, movies, and books; geek nostalgia (especially for 80s children!); conventions, and more. The current writing team consists of six geek ladies and a gay geek guy.

If you are single and looking for a little nudge (or a big one!) to help your dating life, Geek's Dream Girl offers a variety of services. Both E & J are crafty wordsmiths that can make your profile sound just like you wrote it, only shinier. Have a great profile but having a problem taking a relationship from email to the coffee shop? Chat one-on-one with a dating coach that has been there, done that and can give you valuable pointers and a shot of confidence.

Looking to work in the game industry? Geek's Dream Girl hosts a monthly column written by an industry insider to help you achieve – and keep! – your dream job. Since it's often said that the gaming industry is a "boys' club," Geek's Dream Girl showcases the amazing minds of the ladies of the gaming world.

Dice & Deadlines: Freelancing

Hello and welcome to the inaugural column of *Dice & Deadlines*, one woman's perspective on writing for the role-playing game (RPG) industry. As a resident expert on all things RPG related from the inside of the RPG publishing process, I have the honor of pulling back the veil on what it is like to write for the RPG industry and what it means to be a RPG freelance author.

I have written role-playing games since 2004 and have worked with both small and large RPG companies. I've had my share of fumbled rolls by way of bad contracts and critical successes in the form of awards won. I know what outlines mean, how to work with co-workers, when to manage deadline expectations, and where to overwrite my word count. I've leveled up from contributor to co-author to author as well as worked for flat fees, cents per word, and royalties. I have a broad range of experience and I'm ready to share it with you.

Look for the Opportunities

Freelancing for the RPG author is an active thing. You need to look for (or make) the opportunities and grab them. Whether you've completed your twentieth project or you are still looking for your first, a freelance RPG author needs to get out there and actively hunt for those jobs. This means looking at submission guidelines, calls for work, reading forums, talking to other professionals in the business, and doing what needs doing to get the contract.

This is more than just putting your resume out there on the web or on a social networking site and hoping for the best. If you have to start small, do so. I started by reviewing RPG books for *Black Gate* magazine and writing fiction for *Campaign* magazine. I read both magazines and noted in the first one that while they reviewed RPGs, none of the reviewers were women. I emailed the editor and pitched the idea of a female RPG reviewer. He picked me up. In the second, I noted that while they were a gaming magazine, they did not have complimentary fiction as part of their lineup. I emailed them, proposed a fiction line, included my outline, and they hired me.

In both cases, I saw an opportunity to get a foot in the door and I knocked. Neither of these jobs was writing for RPGs but both helped me move into that career.

The Secret of Freelancing is Professionalism

The biggest secret to being a freelance author is to be professional. Freelancing is a job and needs to be treated like a job. Everything about you and what represents you needs to be professional. I'm talking demeanor, dress, business cards (yes, you need them), references, and portfolios. All of this will go a long way to show that you take your job seriously; because if there is one thing I've learned writing for role-playing games, it's that people take their fun very seriously.

The RPG publishing industry is a business. No matter how many people talk about doing it for the love of it, they are also in it for the money or prestige. This means that everyone working for them needs to be professional, good to work with, meet their deadlines, and accept rewrite requests as well as display a myriad of other intangible qualifications.

My final thought on freelancing for the RPG industry is that, by and large, it is a small, incestuous business. Freelancers work for many RPG companies as do editors. Those editors like to talk. They also have long memories. Burning bridges with one editor may end up burning bridges all over the industry. It is best to be polite and professional... and always meet your deadlines.

Dice & Deadlines: Contracts

When writing for any RPG company, you should always have the particulars written out in a contract. This contract should have appropriate names, contact information, the scope of the work, the due date, payment numbers, and the payment schedule. Contracts can be as simple as a one page generic document to a multi-page, super specific, complex monstrosity that includes kill fees, indemnity clauses, royalty payments, publisher guarantees, and various publishing rights, digital rights and foreign rights. It all depends on the company and the scope of the work you are doing for them.

If the RPG company in question will not give you a contract for your work, either you are agreeing to doing the work "on spec" – meaning you write what you write and if they like it then they will give you a contract (usually reserved for tie-in novels) or they are not a professional RPG company who is willing to guarantee, in writing, what they want and what they are willing to pay for it. This latter is best to be avoided.

Payment Pains and Kill Fees

There are a couple of things that you need to look for when examining payment clauses in a contract. The first is "how much"—is the contract correct? The second is "when will I get paid"—after work acceptance or after work publication?

In the first case, contracts are often reused and blanks are filled in and re-filled in over time from contract to contract. If you are not being paid the correct amount (either up or down), you need to not sign the contract and point out the payment error. In the second case, I strongly recommend that you insist that all payment is paid within 30-90 days after work *acceptance* rather than after publication. My first big contract FUBAR involved just that. The publishing company did not publish the work. Thus, I did not get paid and I lost out on several thousand dollars.

If the company insists on payment after the publication of a product, agree only if they will add in a "kill fee" clause to the contract. This is a certain amount of money paid to the freelance author if the project is killed after they have turned in the assignment. The kill fee ensures that you will get paid something for your time and effort. It is not as good as a full payment, but it is certainly better than nothing. It is also a show of good faith on the part of the publishing house that the project will be published and the author will be paid.

Get the idea that sometimes getting paid in the RPG industry is a difficult thing? It is, and a good contract is one way to mitigate the problem.

The Dotted Line

The other thing that a contract does is establish who owns the work after the writing is done and turned in. In most cases, when freelancing for the RPG industry, the publishing house will own it—lock, stock and barrel. This includes all hard copy rights, digital rights, and foreign market rights. If they want to take your work-for-hire fiction and put it all over their website as well as in their product, that is their right as owner of the work. There are rare cases in which this will not apply and you will need to be extra diligent in examining the contract put before you. Your agent (or a lawyer if you don't have an agent) will be able to help you understand what you are signing if it is not a standard contract.

Finally, you need to realize that a contract is a legal, binding document that is there for all parties who sign it. It is there to make sure that the publisher will get the work from the freelance author, to establish the scope and deadline for the work in question, and to assure the author that they will be paid for their effort. You are not just signing a piece of paper. You are promising to make good on your part of the bargain and so is the publishing house.

Dice & Deadlines: The Nitty Gritty

Now that I have talked about freelancing and contracts, it is time to get into the nitty gritty of what it is like to write for an RPG company. There's more to it than just creating awesome worlds for people to immerse themselves in. It's work and comes with its own unique problems.

Playing in Someone Else's Sandbox

The first thing you need to remember is that you are playing in someone else's sandbox. Most of the RPG writing you will do as freelancer will be in already established worlds with set rules for everything from weapons to magic to using skills. Moreover, you are writing in a world that someone out there loves beyond life itself and they will (I promise you) know if you mess up in any way. If you mess up a stat, a rule, a name, an ability, a border, or how a person of a particular religious order pours a drink for someone of a higher station, they *will* know.

Then you get angry forum posts about how you ruined the game.

In an attempt to mitigate this problem before it begins, many companies have databases, wikis, and FTP repositories of information and previously published books. When it comes to long standing companies with RPG worlds that have been around for decades, this is the only way to maintain continuity. When writing for

an established game world, continuity is your
friend. It is the RPG author's duty to maintain
that continuity at all times. Never hesitate to
consult with your peers if you are uncertain
about a fact.

Outlines and Word Counts

Next come the technical particulars of your
contract—and you *do* have a contract, don't
you? This usually comes in the form of an
outline or a spreadsheet with section headers
and word counts on them. What's this mean? It
means that you need to write 400 words on
why a person would worship an evil god, 200
words on a new type of monster and 1,500
words on the opening fiction for a chapter. You
must write what is needed and you must meet
your word count.

Outlines are used more often when the RPG
author is assigned a large section of a book.
This will detail chapter sub-headings, word
counts, flavor text sections and example
adventures. However, the RPG author needs to
be flexible. I have had both the detailed outline
with an overall word count with section break
downs and word counts and I have had a single
chapter title heading with a word count and
nothing else. I looked at how previous chapters
were broken out and mimicked that. Again,
continuity.

When it comes to word counts, industry practice allows a 10% overwrite for a section. However, as an editor, and talking to other editors, you should never, ever underwrite your assigned section in a book. It is easier to cut words than to add them. From experience, you will get an intuitive understanding for how long a certain number of words is and be able to write to near that length on a first draft.

As an aside, on my first contract for one company I hit every word count exactly and freaked out the editor. That's when I discovered the 10% overwriting practice. Sometimes, it *is* the little things that count.

Fundamental Understandings

Finally, there is an intangible thing you need to understand when it comes to writing in an established world. You need to understand the feel of what has gone before and maintain that feel. If the RPG is horror, you don't introduce camp. If the RPG is a comedy, you don't attempt to be serious. You keep to the path when you are working in someone else's world. Your new blood is there to give the RPG new life but not take away from what is already there.

When I am hired to write in a new RPG that I am unfamiliar with (something I don't really recommend), I try to get into that RPG. I make a character. If I can, I coax someone who is already familiar with the established setting into running a game for me. I learn what I can through game play, and I try to take away what it is that the established fan base of the setting loves about it. With this experience, I think I do a better job at writing in that world.

Dice & Deadlines: Deadlines and Extensions

Since I talked last time about the nitty-gritty of RPG writing and some of the trials of writing in another's RPG universe creation—or 'playing in someone else's sandbox' if you will—I wanted to talk about a couple of things that every single writer will face: meeting and missing deadlines.

Why Are Deadlines So Important?

In *Dice & Deadlines: Freelancing*, I talked about the RPG industry being a business. Publishers are in it because they want to make money first. They love the business of role-playing games second. This is especially true when dealing with the major players in the RPG arena—Wizards of the Coast, CCP, Pathfinder, Fantasy Flight Games and numerous others. They all have to answer to the bottom line. And you, as a freelancer, do affect that bottom line.

A Typical Schedule

Gen Con Indy, scheduled for August, is one of the major annual gaming conventions in the United States. It is one of several. A large number of companies schedule their major launches for conventions like Gen Con Indy. In order for that RPG book to be presented at the convention, the timeline (very roughly) looks something like this:

- December/January – Freelancers receive assignment and contract.
- February – Freelancers turn in assignment, get feedback and rewrite requests.
- March – Final freelance work to editor for last edits and editor gives the whole book a final edit.
- April – Book to layout editor and then to a final round of proofing.
- May – Book to printer, receive proof, send back with changes, and receive new proof.
- June – Accepted final proof of book to printer.
- August – Book launch along with author signings and swag giveaways.

Look tight? It is. That is the name of the game when it comes to writing for the RPG industry; a lot of writing with tight turnarounds. So, what happens if you slip or miss your deadline? Everything gets moved out, some other freelancer gets picked up to finish what you didn't, the editor does the work. The book slipping its schedule and missing its launch date will cost the company time and money.

No matter what, no one is happy. Not the editor who chose you and ended up with extra work. Not the company who lost money. Not you because your reputation is tarnished.

When to Ask for an Extension

Now, not every book is scheduled to release on a convention but every book release has a specific release date for a reason—quarter end, RPG creation anniversary, you name it. But we all know life happens. Slips happen. When do you request an extension?

As soon as you realize you will not hit your deadline and not a moment later.

I was given three months to write a 70,000 word Savage Worlds book; more than enough time for me. I finished another project during that first month and started the book in the second month. At the end of that second month, a friend of mine died and left me reeling. By the time I pulled myself back together, I knew I would not make that deadline and I knew that, as the sole author on the book, I needed an extension. As soon as I realized it, I did what I needed to do.

How to Ask for an Extension

I did ask for the extension. But before I wrote that email, I did my homework. I figured out how much I had left to do, how many words I could get done in a day and figured out how much time I needed. So, my email told the publisher what happened in short, professional terms, that I needed an extension and how long that extension needed to be.

When you need to go to your boss (that is who your editor or publisher is) with your hat in your hands, you will look 100% better if you have done your due diligence and can ask for exactly what you need. This gives the company enough information to determine if they have the time to give you or if they need to pull in a pinch hitter.

The moral of the story is to always meet your deadlines. If you can't do that, inform the company immediately and ask for an extension of a specific length of time.

Dice & Deadlines: Rewrites

Previously on *Dice & Deadlines* I talked about meeting deadlines and asking for extensions. Every RPG project has an editor. Ditto with every fiction project. An editor's job is to make the product and the author(s) look as good as possible. *Every author needs an editor.* I mean it. From your favorite blockbuster on the NYT Bestsellers List right down to the smallest Indie RPG author out there. Every single one. Me included.

After your manuscript is turned in, the editor of the product looks at it and edits it. An editor does three types of edits: line edits, copy edits, and proofing. Line editing is editing for tone, style, and consistency with the core product. Copy editing is editing to improve the formatting, grammar, and accuracy of the text. Proofing is editing to find and correct technical production mistakes in the final copy of the product. And to fix any typos that bred in the process.

The freelancer's job continues after line edits when the editor returns the marked up manuscript for rewrites—which are manuscript change requests from the editor to the author to fix continuity mistakes, smooth over rough prose, and shift the tone to fit the product line's core.

Handling Rewrites for Short Gigs

Short writing gigs of 10,000 words or less
usually don't have significant rewrite
requests—if you get any at all. You may need to
fix continuity errors that cropped up because it
conflicted with a part of the book you didn't
work on. Most likely, you will be asked to trim
your word count.

New freelancers to an RPG company may get a
copy of their edited manuscript with tracked-
changes enabled as a visual teaching method to
show how the editor likes things in the future.
This is not an attack on you as an author. This
is a much-needed exchange between the editor
and the author. Editors are our friends. Believe
me on this one.

Most of the time, you won't get any rewrite
requests for short gigs. You will turn in your
work, have it accepted and the editor will
massage the text to fit their vision of the overall
product. Remember, the freelancer is doing
commission work. It is not "original fiction"
because you are playing in someone else's
sandbox and whatever you write must fit into
that mold. Personally, I count it as a win when
I don't get back a rewrite request.

Handling Rewrites for Long Gigs

When it comes to longer writing gigs for the
RPG industry, turning in pieces of the
manuscript early is a good thing. It is not
always required but is sometimes necessary.
When I wrote *Proverbial Monsters* for White
Wolf, I turned in the completed manuscript at
33,000 words and received a decent amount of
rewrites to do. Almost 100% of these rewrites
were to massage the manuscript into a true
World of Darkness product with the
appropriate feel.

Several of the monster powers were modified to
fit White Wolf rules. Some of the background
had to be truncated because I wrote too much
and many of my monsters were renamed. I was
originally miffed by this. However, they were
renamed by a linguistics specialist on the White
Wolf staff. Thus, not only did they fit better into
the product line universe, they had a linguist's
backing—making the product that much better.
Obviously, I got over my pique. And that's what
you need to do as well.

I was very lucky with *Proverbial Monsters*.
When I wrote *Millennium Knights* for Savage
Mojo, I turned in a 77,000 word manuscript
and wound up having to completely rewrite a
22,000 word section—lock, stock, and barrel—
because I completely missed a significant point
in the way Savage Mojo wrote that part of the
book. To be fair, I wrote that book very quickly
and turned in sections of the book while the

editor was both sick and traveling. It was the perfect storm of missing each other so that he never had the chance to halt me before I had gone too far in the wrong direction.

These things do happen and as such you just have to roll with them. While you can discuss change requests with the editor, at the end of the day, you are paid to make the editor happy and the editor's word is law.

Dice & Deadlines: Multiple Authors, One Product

I've talked about a number of different things that a freelancer needs to be aware of when writing for the RPG industry: deadlines, extensions, rewrites, professionalism, and contracts. All of that is based on either you the author or your relationship with the editor. But, if you open an RPG book and look at the credits page, you often see many names credited as "game designer" or "additional words." This is because most RPG books are written by more than one freelancer.

Why there are multiple authors on a single product often comes down to time and effort. The RPG industry works on a very fast schedule. Most RPG core books are between 75,000 and 120,000 words. Most people cannot write that much in the allotted time. Thus, pieces are broken out into sections. It is much easier to write 30,000 publishable words in a month than 90,000 in three months. Burn out is always a danger.

Also, it comes down to skill sets. One freelancer may be excellent at world building but suck at doing stats. Another may be a math nerd, excelling at stats and all the crunchy bits of an RPG but couldn't write their way through an introductory scene. An experienced editor knows what her freelancers can do and makes assignments accordingly.

The Co-Author

Frequently, RPG books will have just two authors. That means these authors need to work together to make the book the best it can be. My experience has been when it is a co-authorship, one author is the expert in the IP and the other is an 'up-and-comer' as they say. In this case, the roles will be clear. The expert is in charge and the other freelancer works with them. All questions about the IP go to the expert. If you are not the expert, you need to be able to work with the expert and expand upon what they say.

Another co-authorship I've encountered is one with a clear delineation of tasks. On *Shanghai Vampocalypse*, I was the sole fiction author. I was responsible for all of the world building, plots, monster description, and canon characters. My co-author was responsible for all of the crunchy stats. I described the monster, the weapon or the character and made a note about the power level and he wrote up the appropriate Savage Worlds stats for it. This was where my descriptions and my production notes had to be especially clear. I wrote my part and then threw it over the wall to my co-author.

The final co-authorship I've been a part of is the equal partner method where sections of the book are divvied up, each author writes their section, and then the co-author edits it before the product editor ever looks at the work. This process involves the most communication and collaboration between the authors. Each author needs to know their own strengths and weaknesses and to fill in where the co-author lacks.

Over the Wall Never to be Seen Again...Until Production

Many multi-authored products do not have any contact between authors unless they are in-house authors. Most of the time, you will get your piece of the pie and that's it. You will write it to specification, send it up the line, and never see it again until the book comes out in production.

What do you do then? You do the best you can with what you have based on the history of the product in question. You use the resources the company gives you, you meet your word count, you meet your deadline and you do your rewrites. That is all you can do.

Writing by Committee

Depending on the company you work for, you may encounter "writing by committee." This is where a group of freelancers has been commissioned to work on a single product. Everyone gets their pieces of the book and as each finishes a section, they upload it to a site for the rest of the freelancers to see, critique, and build upon in their sections. It's collaboration between the freelancers and the editor.

This is one of the most daunting and rewarding ways to write an RPG book; it allows for mistakes to be caught early and design features to be spread throughout the product. After reading everyone else's work, the writing you do on your section of the book meshes better with everyone else. It brings cohesion to the book that other products often do not have.

This style of game design is not for the weak hearted or thin-skinned. Freelancers are passionate, opinionated people and you will need to know how to hold your own while being professional.

Editor Trumps All

Remember, no matter if you have just two authors working on a product or ten, the editor must ride herd over them all. It is the editor's job to make sure that the product is consistent in tone and genre, concise and correct in information, and generally entertaining. While you have your pie of the product, the editor has the 50,000 foot view of what's really going on— now and in the future.

Dice & Deadlines: Convention Networking

I've talked a lot about how the freelancer works within the RPG industry. Contracts, word counts, professionalism, editors, and co-authors. But there is more to being a freelancer than just writing. Much more. It's called networking. And that's what I'm going to focus on for the next few articles.

Don't let the term "networking" give you hives. Really, all it means is going out, talking to people, and making contacts within the industry. This particular article is going to focus specifically on gaming conventions and professionalism—especially when dealing with other RPG professionals. I'm not going to talk about the freelancer personally (hygiene and such) because Jess Hartley has one of the best and least expensive resources out there. Check out *Conventions for the Aspiring Game Professional* on DriveThruRPG.com.

I'm going to talk about some of the less obvious nuances that will help you connect with the people you want to connect with.

Timing and Opportunity

The first thing you need to realize is that your timing is the most important part of social networking. Interrupting another professional while they are in a meeting, a meal, with family, or something else where they are clearly busy is not a good idea. If you are remembered, you will not be remembered for the right reasons. Thus, you must pick out the ideal times and grab opportunities where you can.

Some of the best times to approach a professional are "transitional" periods: Asking to walk with them to their next panel, after a group of people has left their dealers table, as they head out for food (but don't invite yourself to the meal) and so on. One of my more fortunate meetings was in the line waiting for coffee. Another one was waiting for a panel to start.

The key to meeting people is timing but the grease that keeps the social wheels turning is being able to gracefully accept a rejection. Frequently, professionals will not have time, even in the transitional periods, to talk to you. If you request time and they turn you down, accepting that without fuss will go a long way for the next time you try to meet up.

In The Dealers Room

Networking in the Dealers Room is both the best and worst time to do it at a convention. Frequently, the person you want to talk to (the editor, the line developer) is a captive audience behind a table at a booth. This means you know where they are. However, this is their job and you absolutely must allow them to work: selling their product, talking to their writers, and so forth.

That said, there are often down time moments where the savvy freelancer can slip in and talk to their target. Always have a business card. Always ask for a business card. If it is an editor I do not know, I usually start with, *"Hello. I'm Jennifer Brozek. I'm a freelance author and I was wondering if you were looking for more freelancers for your product."* It is that simple. Be prepared to talk about what you have worked on and what you like about the product you want to write for. If they say no, thank them for their time and move on.

At all times during your conversation with the person behind the dealers table, you must be prepared to step to the side and allow the RPG professional to do the job of selling their product to people who come to the table. Patience is a virtue and it may be the key to getting you a job.

Parties: Sponsored and Otherwise

Parties have become a big part of conventions. Sponsored parties are usually thrown by one of the larger companies attending the convention. Frequently, these parties will have required invitations or tickets to attend. How one receives these invites is all based upon the individual company. Some are much stricter than others. Some, you just have to 'know a guy.' In the end, if you get in, you get to party with some of the greats in the industry.

One thing to remember though: people in the RPG industry work hard and they like to play hard. But, that is no excuse for you to become a sloppy drunk. They will not appreciate you vomiting on their shoes while you try to pitch yourself to them as a freelancer.

Non-sponsored parties are usually much harder to get into if you don't know someone who is already going. They are rumored to be like the fabled "after parties" of Hollywood. In truth, they are usually a bunch of tired convention RPG professionals who just want to sit and drink in quiet while sharing a companionable word. If you are invited into one of these parties, be on your best behavior.

BarCon: the Con Within a Con

Didn't get an invite to a sponsored party? Didn't 'know a guy' who could get you into something more private? Don't worry. At all conventions, there is the convention within the convention: BarCon. This is the bar (or bars depending on how big the convention is) where many of the professionals go to hang out when they need a break or food. This is, by design, supposed to be an open and social thing where people come and go. New people and old friends congregate to tell "no shit, there I was" stories of the RPG or real life varieties.

Circulating at BarCon can be daunting but, if you've been around at the convention, visited the dealers room, or gone to the panels, there will be people you recognize. If they are at the bar, unless they are off in a corner looking intense and business-like, it is OK to go up and say hello. But don't immediately pitch yourself. Just relax and enjoy. Talk about your pets, your games, your friends, that cool purchase, or whatever. Eventually, people will start asking you questions about you. It's part of human nature. *Then* you can let them know that not only are you a freelancer, you are open for new work. If they are interested, they'll ask for a business card.

You do have your business cards, don't you?

After the Con

Making a connection is only one part of the deal at a convention. The grips and grins help get your foot in the door but you still have to close the deal and that means following up after the convention. One to two weeks after the convention, go through your stack of business cards and email all of the ones you said you would get back to. Thank them for the meeting, express your interest in their product, and remind them how they met you and what you can do for them. Networking is always about the follow through. That's where the actual jobs come from.

Dice & Deadlines: Public Relations

Part of your job as a freelancer for the RPG industry is to have a public face. This is all part of the networking you do to keep track of the pulse of the RPG world. Public relations, in the context of this article, are all about how you deal with the public who consume your work and the industry who hires you to produce that work.

For this article, I am going to focus primarily on the face to face aspect of public relations management. Next month's article will focus on the internet aspect of the deal.

Face to Face: Keeping Your Suit On

When in the public eye, the rule to follow is: Keep your suit on in public and cry in private. This means to present a professional look and demeanor. A neat appearance and a calm expression will go a long way. Keeping things civil in the face of adversity, farce or confusion will garner the best results for you and your reputation.

When it comes to the public, anything can happen. People will ask for autographs on their books (I recommend a signature that is *not* like the one you use for writing checks), pictures of you with them (the value of a neat appearance), and they will want to talk to you about all sorts of things. How you deal with them will be remembered.

Patience and politeness is the key. Even if you need to deny a request, leave the area or continue with business. A cordial response, "No, I'm sorry, I cannot read your manuscript due to contractual obligations," will be received much better even if it is not the desired answer.

Mistakes, They Do Happen

When it comes to mistakes, be prepared for them to happen. Be it misspeaking, getting someone's name wrong, being late or any of the thousands of other things that can and will happen. It is best to acknowledge it, apologize for it, fix it if you can and move on. Dwelling on a mistake you made (and are aware you made) will not help you or the situation.

Sometimes, it is hard to admit you made a mistake. Swallowing your ego and pride is never an easy thing. However, I have discovered that nothing stops bad press in its tracks like a sincere apology. Also, everyone makes mistakes. If you catch someone making a mistake in regards to you, think about how you would want it handled if the shoe were on the other foot and react accordingly.

Yes, keeping your suit on really does mean treat people as you would like them to treat you.

To Respond or Not To Respond

There will be times in your career where you will be called out on something you did or wrote. They will often feel like personal attacks. Sometimes they are. Sometimes they aren't. And sometimes, the people attacking your work are just looking for attention. You always have a choice on whether or not you will respond and how.

Personal attacks: Sometimes, people will say inflammatory things to you in person while you are at the dealer's booth, during a reading, or at a book signing. Your best bet is to let the event organizer deal with them. Or your handler or that good friend you have with you for just such an occasion. If they want to have a real dialogue with you, determine if it is the time or place. If they don't, your best bet is not to respond.

Panels: Frequently, while you are at a convention on a panel, you will be challenged on what you say or think by the audience or the other panel members. If the challenge is not within the scope of the panel, say so and ask for the next question. If it is, answer it as professionally as you can. It is possible to have a cordial disagreement with someone based on experience. Frequently, spirited discussions are the most interesting thing about panels as long as they remain professional.

Online: I will spend a lot more time on this next month but, by and large, if someone calls you out on the internet—lambasts an opinion, gives a bad review, etc—your best bet is not to respond. At all. Humor does not translate well. Explanations can be nitpicked to death and, generally, no matter what you do, you will not win.

In the end, if you are a professional, you will be treated as one. Even if people disagree with you. You are allowed to have emotions but there is a time and place for them. Keeping your suit on in public is one of the best ways of managing your professional reputation.

Dice & Deadlines: Your Internet Presence

There is the real world of brick and mortar and then there is the internet world. This is the world of blogs, boards, instant messenger, Twitter, Facebook, and a thousand other social media websites. Digital real estate is booming and those who know how to manipulate it are cashing in. Even those of us who are comfortable behind the screen can get lost in the crowd where flame wars are the norm and spam is a daily occurrence.

Why is an Internet Presence Important?

One of the main reasons having a solid internet presence is important is that it allows you, the author, to reach more people. These are the people who buy the products you create or contribute to. These are also the people who make the decisions on who to hire next.

My internet presence spans websites (professional), blogs (personal and professional), Facebook (personal and fan page), Twitter (Yes), instant messenger, and a myriad of email addresses to help organize my life. 100% of my jobs are remote. This means I get 100% of my income from my contact on the internet. I may meet people at conventions but it is the digital follow up that gets me the job.

I have given people work through Twitter as well as been solicited for work through Twitter, Facebook and Livejournal. Without a solid internet presence, these jobs would never have happened.

Part Marketing, Part You

The first thing you need to realize is that while your internet presence is you, it is also a marketing tool. It cannot be one or the other. It needs to be both. No one wants to constantly read "buy my stuff." Also, if all you have on your blog is pictures of your pet llama and nothing about your writing, prospective readers, editors, and publishers will have no idea that you are an author or what you write. Thus, you must balance the marketing with the personal.

In my blogs, I separate the two. In one, it is all personal (cats, husband, gaming, chores, etc...) with hints of the professional. In the professional blog, I have announcements of sales, what I'm working on, when things are released and events I'm attending. But, I also have personal writing advice based on my experience. I link in personal things that happen to me that inspire, help or hinder my writing. I am professional but I am also personable.

There are some people who have excelled at having an excellent online presence that balances personal and professional lives. John

Scalzi, Cherie Priest, Cat Rambo, Jay Lake, and the King of Geeks, Wil Wheaton... not to mention the ever grumpy but highly talented Warren Ellis. Look up any of these people and read what they have to say. You will learn about both their professional and personal lives as well as see how they present their products while remaining a real person.

But People are Wrong on the Internet

And here we come to the sticky part of the equation. The internet is filled with landmines and those landmines are known as people. There are trolls in these there woods. Trolls, opinionated assholes, pricks who are right, reviewers, readers, editors, publishers, lovers, haters and, in general, most of the world. Trust me when I say that your mere presence on the internet will upset someone while another person will thank the stars above.

Everything you write on the internet is read by someone. Never assume that what you post online is private. Even if it is 'behind locked doors' because people are a wild card. Some will be good for your career. Some will be bad. And some won't care one way or the other as long as they are getting attention.

People are wrong on the internet. This is a fact. An author will never win a flame war. This is my opinion. They may be right against their opponent but they will still come off with a bad reputation in the end. Even if a reviewer lambasts your book because it is exactly what it says it is (and I speak from personal experience), it is best not to respond. No matter how angry it makes you because, on the whole, the RPG publishing industry is small and the toes you step on today may belong to the ass you need to kiss tomorrow.

Dice & Deadlines: Expanding Your Horizons

When it comes to the RPG industry, there are only so many open positions. Those game designers with experience and reputation will acquire those jobs before the inexperienced or less well known. Of course there is balance between cost of the game designer and the job to be done. Every company is looking for the next big idea along with the next big author.

One way to get over the hump of scarcity of game design jobs is to expand your horizons—and your skill set—and do other jobs in the industry. The well rounded freelancer is one who will never lack for work as long as they do a good job in every position they accept.

You as a Game Designer

There are several different jobs you can do as a Game Designer. There is the world builder—who creates the setting, the lands, the description of the political or religious hierarchy, and the relationship between competing factions. There is the fiction RPG writer—who creates the flavor text, the opening stories, and sets the general atmosphere of the book. There is the Numbers person—this invaluable game designer is the one who sets the stats for the monsters, NPCs, weapons, and equipment.

Most of the time, if you work in the industry, you must be able to world build. That is the bulk of the writing. However, the most important person is the one who can work the numbers and stat out everything that needs stats. For a long time, I only did world building and fiction writing for RPGs. I was not confident enough in my own abilities to do the numbers.

Then, I received a full book contract. The work included doing all the stats. I was not going to turn the contract down because I "could not" do statting. I worked hard, learned from others, and did what needed doing. After that, I was more confident and I was able to take on the jobs that included the numbers and thus made myself a more valuable freelancer.

You as a Fiction Author

Straight up fiction writing is not world building. While you do world build, you are really telling a story that a reader—who may or may not know the RPG world—will enjoy. This kind of writing requires a different set of skills. Most RPG game designers are also fiction writers, but not all.

Having the ability to write a good story will open up different freelancing avenues like tie-in anthologies, novels, or website serials. Knowing the RPG world that you are writing fiction in lends itself to making these stories that much richer and exciting to the RPG aficionado while not confusing the reader who is just looking for a good story.

You as an Editor

I have said this before but I will say it again:
everyone needs an editor. This is especially true
in the RPG industry. Editors make the products
flow together in a single, cohesive piece of art.
They are the overall polisher who smoothes
over different writing styles from different
authors into something without jarring
transitions.

Also, editors catch mistakes—logical mistakes,
factual mistakes, historical mistakes, and any
other kind of mistake an author can make. This
makes a game designer, who can switch hats
into an editor, a freelancer who is in demand. I
understand we all want to be writers but a
writer who can also professionally edit will
become a better writer as well as keep
themselves on the payroll. It is a skill set worth
developing.

You as a Blogger/Marketer/PR

There will be times when there are no game
design or editing jobs available but there are
the necessary jobs that involve marketing RPG
products or authors of those products. Having
the ability to shift to a professional blogger,
reviewer, or marketer can bring in money.
There are RPG companies out there who will
pay for professional writing quality reviews for
their website, or for blogger essays on topics
related to their products. Also, everything you

read on the internet—be it a product description, a book blurb, or back cover copy—is written by someone who was paid to do it. Think about that.

Expanding your skill set to become a multitalented writer and editor is one way to ensure that you receive consistent work as a freelancer. There are a number of jobs related to being a game designer that allow the freelancer to do more, get paid more, and to discover what else it is they like to do. If you have the opportunity to learn multiple jobs, I encourage you do to so.

Dice & Deadlines: Just Ask and Share the Love

I am often asked, "How do you get your freelance jobs?" My response usually is, "I ask for them or someone recruits me for them." This leads to a series of questions around how I ask for jobs or how people know to recruit me. Somehow, despite my introverted nature and shy tendencies, I have become fearless when it comes to freelancing. This is how I do it.

Just Ask—the Worst They Can Do is Say No

The idea of networking used to give me hives. As it turns out, "networking" is talking to people in the industry, being pleasant, and letting it be known that you are available for work. My perspective of being a freelancer means I must take a more active role in getting freelance gigs. I have to go digging for them and tell my prospective clients that I want the job they have open.

This leads me to my first big point: Just ask. Go to the publisher you have always wanted to work with and ask them if they have any freelance gigs available or if they keep a pool of freelancers on file for when the gigs are available. The worst they can do is say no. Thank them and move on. Or not. You can stay and talk with them about their product. Just be aware that asking will often get you told "no" or "not right now" and that's okay. There are other companies out there.

If you keep coming back and you are pleasant in your demeanor, eventually, they might say, "Yes."

Holes Are Opportunities

Sometimes, you have to make your own opportunities to get a freelance job. I do this by listening to what is big in the industry or what direction the RPG industry is moving in and see if I can leverage that. Forward thinking is a good thing. For example, I listened to a publisher at GenCon talk about how PDF was the next big wave of publication. From there, I thought about a company I wanted to work with and looked at what their PDF product line was like. Then, I looked to see what they *didn't* have. In this case, a series of PDF settings—small products they could put out in-between their large hardcopy products. Then I met with the publisher and pitched him the idea of including such smaller products with lower overhead and a higher profit margin.

This is just one example of how you, as a freelancer, can make your own opportunities in this industry. Look at the games you play, what you wish you could have as a gamer, and do your research. Chances are, you could start a whole new revenue stream for you and for the company you contact.

You Don't Have to Fail for Me to Succeed

You ever hear that saying, "What goes around, comes around?" It basically means that you will get back what you put out in the world. This is something I believe. Thus, I have a "share the love" policy. If I can help someone else succeed, someday they will help me succeed.

I do not consider being a freelancer to be a competition. There is not only one. You don't have to lose for me to win. Because game design is often a collaborative effort, I want as many people I know and like to work with me as I can. If I can give you some good advice, I will. If I can give you a heads up on a call for submissions, I will. This industry is small and most people will remember a good turn and repay that effort in a similar manner.

You are not going to like everyone you work with or are a peer to. Expecting that is setting yourself up to fail. However, politeness and courtesy go a very long way. Treat your peers the way you want to be treated... and share the love. You will enjoy what you get back in the long run.

Dice & Deadlines: Know When to Say When

The hardest thing in the world is for the freelancer to turn down a paying job. There will be times when this is a necessity. The worst thing a freelancer can do for their career and professional reputation is to accept a contract and then blow the deadline. You should only accept a contract if you know you can complete it in the allotted time.

When Should You Turn Down a Job?

It is your responsibility to know when you should turn down a job. There are a couple of ways you can determine this. This is how I do it: I look at all my due dates and the word count due on those dates. I calculate the minimum amount of good, publishable words I need to produce per day to make my deadline. Then, I add in the amount of research I will need to do to complete my job and then add in the lost days I know I will have if I am traveling during that time.

If I can look at that number of words per day and not wince, I'm doing good. I keep a queue going of all of my contracted jobs in a document I look at every single day. I remain aware of my obligations and as job offers come in, I weigh my current obligations against the incoming work and see if I still can do it.

The moment I look at that word count per day and pause, not sure if I can do it, I either turn the job down with regret or I ask if the due date can be moved out to a date that accommodates my current schedule. I will not take on a job I cannot finish.

Figure out your productivity level and schedule accordingly.

Refreshing the Well

There will be times in your professional career where you will hate your job and the idea of writing another word will seem like torture. When you hit this point of burnout (or, preferably before it), you need to pause and refresh the creative well. The only way you can do that is to not write and go do something else. Something that inspires and pleases you. Something that gives your creative writing mind a rest while refilling it with new ideas and new motivation.

Refreshing the well can happen for an afternoon, a day, or, you could need to take a week away from the work. Go read books for fun. Go to the museum. Change your physical location or just give yourself permission to sleep in and play videogames. All work and no play is detrimental to the freelancer. We all need time to relax and relax that creative muscle.

I frequently take a few days in-between long projects to do nothing. I allow myself the time to refresh the well and, thus, have a much more energetic and fresh approach to the new project.

Know When to Say When

Repeat clients and ongoing jobs are the bread and butter of a freelance writer's life. Regular columns, serial fiction, and consistent monthly world building are ideal jobs for the freelancer—until they're not. There will come a time when that regular magazine essay becomes just a job and not the joy that it used to be. And as hard as this will be, that is the point in which the freelancer needs to step back from the consistent, regular, repeating work and resign.

It may be nothing more than a lack of time or having said all you want to say that tells you it is time to "say when." Such is the case with me. I have a number of new projects coming up and not as much time as I would like for this column, *Dice & Deadlines*. That means this is my last column. However, it does not mean the end of *Dice & Deadlines*. **Geek's Dream Girl** is continuing *Dice & Deadlines* with a new RPG insider. I know who she is and I think you all are going to enjoy her perspective for the next year as much as I will enjoy reading her column.

This is farewell. Feel free to look me up on the web. I have had a marvelous time over the last year with Geek's Dream Girl and *Dice &*

Deadlines but I know when to say when and that time is now. Thank you all for reading.

*RPGirl: Role Playing Girl magazine is an
anthology of essays by and about women who
play role-playing games. I wrote this article for
RPGirl Zine, published in August 2010.
Reprinted in Italian in 2011 by Gioco Da
Ragazze.*

RPGirl Zine Article: RPG Freelancing is an Active Thing

Author, RPG world builder, editor, proofer.
There are days when I feel like I am a writing
industry Swiss Army knife. There are so many
pies and I have my fingers in a lot of them.
People ask me how I do it and, more
importantly, why I do it.

There is no one simple answer, but I will tell
you why I do what I do. First, and foremost, a
freelancer in the writing industry lives and dies
by her contracts. No contracts, no recognition,
no money. This will just not do for me. The
second, and no less important answer, is that I
like to do all of these different jobs. They
exercise different parts of my brain and give the
other parts a rest.

Fiction writing is very different from RPG
writing. Most fiction writing I do, I get to pour
out of my brain and onto the page through
flying fingers. I get to make the rules, break
them, fix them, and generally decide where the
story is going and what is going to happen. The
only consideration is keeping in mind what

came before and if I am writing in a universe I've written in previously. There is a freedom in the storytelling that I cannot describe but sincerely appreciate.

RPG writing is much more structured. When creating a world or writing in a previously established RPG universe, there is so much more to be careful of—established people, places, and things. When I worked on the *Big Damn Heroes Handbook* by Margaret Weis Productions, I had to remember that, not only were there previously established TV episodes, comic books, and a movie to consider, there were legions of loyal fans who would have my head if I got any part of it wrong. Fortunately, Cam Banks, the editor of that book, kept all of the authors in canon and on track.

When I write RPGs in an established universe like *Colonial Gothic* by Rogue Games, I have less media tie-ins to worry about and much more freedom to explore the game universe on my own. My only limitations are the previously written work and, well, American history. I love writing this kind of RPG because, in a way, it is like getting paid to write fan fiction that becomes canon. I wrote two PDF settings, *Colonial Gothic: Elizabethtown* and *Colonial Gothic: Plymouth,* in which I got to write everything about the towns, using their actual history as story fodder. It was my idealized version of playing the "what if" game.

Editing and proofing work is an entirely
different animal. You must approach it with a
completely different mindset. Not only are you
looking for a good story or concise world
building, you are looking for consistency in
word usage, verb tense, number formulation
and a myriad of other nitpicky formatting
details that determine the difference between
an understandable, well written book and one
that is not. Every publishing company I have
worked for has had a slightly different way of
going about their editing and proofing. Smart
companies have a style guide that the editors
(heck, the authors, too) can refer back to. It is
one of the first things an author or editor
should ask for when working with a new-to-
them company.

Not every author can do all of these jobs and
many do not want to. That is fine. In fact,
better than fine as it allows the author or editor
to work to their strengths and that makes for a
better product. Once you know and hone your
strengths—fiction writing, world building,
editing—it is time to get to work.

One of the most asked questions I receive is:
"How did you get into RPG writing?" This
question usually has the underlying query of
"How can I getting into RPG writing?" My
answer is the same answer I use to *keep*
writing in the RPG industry: I present my
credentials and I asked if the publisher has any
open gigs.

That's the short version.

The longer version of what I do is to go to conventions, meet industry people, try to keep up on who is doing what, and keep my eyes open for opportunities. But, the important point is that I ask. I make contact. I follow submission guidelines. For me, freelancing is an *active* thing. I do the work of getting the jobs and then I do them as well as I can. That keeps me working.

Remember the PDF settings for *Colonial Gothic*? Rogue Games did not have such a product out, but keeping a pulse on the RPG industry told me that this was an emerging market. I wanted to work for Rogue Games, so I went to the publisher and I proposed the PDF setting concept, complete with outline and word count. Obviously, they accepted the idea and later contracted me to do the second one. (Update: As of this book, I have written five PDF settings and co-authored a novella for Rogue Games.) I would not have gotten any of these jobs if I had not taken the risk and asked.

I think my single most important business tool, beyond getting out there for grips and grins with the publishers, is to have an appropriate business card to hand over. This card is the thing that will represent you when you are not there. It should be clean and professional with appropriate contact information. The back should be plain and non-glossy so the publisher (or you) can write notes about what you two talked about. And after you have handed off your business card, always ask for one in return. Finally, follow up with the publisher within two weeks after the meeting.

It all seems so simple: figure out your strengths, hone your skills, ask for the work and follow up with any contacts you make. It's not. All of it requires constant upkeep and consistently excellent work. This means hours of work outside of the actual acts of writing or editing. Freelancing is a commitment, a time sink, and often, a thankless job. However, for me, seeing that product out on the shelves as a best seller makes it all worth it.

Juggling Chain Saws: How to Manage a Freelance Career Schedule

One of the most frequent questions I get asked after "When do you sleep?" is "How do you keep track of all your projects?" This latter question boils down to two questions: "How do you juggle multiple projects?" and "How do you make sure you hit your deadlines with so much going on?"

The answer to the first question is that I do project management on myself all the time. Beyond keeping an excellent up-to-date spreadsheet of current projects and due dates, whenever I am asked to take on a new project, I ask myself three questions:

"How much time will this take?"

How much time something will take is more than just word count. I can write very quickly when I am inspired and I have a free rein. However, some projects require a lot more work beyond "just writing." This work can include historical research, combing through years worth of IP on a particular product, and figuring out all of math for the statistics required. The more I have to do beyond "just writing," the more time it will take me. I need to factor in all of the time for the job. 10,000 words of fiction for one project could take three weeks instead of three days.

"How much money will I spend/make?"

Freelance writing and editing is my job. It is a business. I need to keep that in forefront of my mind. This means I need to look at cold hard numbers associated with a job. How much will I be paid? Do I need to purchase anything to get the job done? If it is for charity, I need to think long and hard to see if it will fit into my schedule. At this point in my career, I rarely work for free. However, I will do so if I believe the cause is worth it and it fits into my schedule.

"What am I willing to give up to do this project?"

This is the squishy emotional part of the equation. I look at due dates, what I already have in the queue, how much I want to work with the company in question, and what I will need to give up to add the new project to my ever expanding list.

Most often, what is sacrificed for a writing assignment is entertainment. I must severely limit my TV watching and book reading. It is the loss of reading that hurts more than the loss of TV. I frequently don't see movies until they come out on Netflix. I do not play any MMOs because when I do, they tend to take over my life for a time and kill my writing productivity.

On the other hand, downtime is important for writers. I need time to play and recharge. I cannot cut out all of my downtime—even for a cool project—because that way lies madness and burn out. Work and play must balance out.

Listen to Your Gut

Once I answer and rate each project in a queue, I then listen to my emotional gut whine about what I want to do more. Want sometimes wins out over practicality. Sometimes I will sacrifice a week's worth of playtime in order to add in a new project to my schedule. Sometimes I won't. If I am wincing at where the deadline due dates are in conjunction with the number of publishable words I need to produce in a given time, I must have the fortitude to decline the job due to too many deadlines.

As much as it may pain you to turn down a job, keeping a good handle on your work queue is the best thing you can do for all involved. Time management means knowing your limits and remembering, in the end, freelancing is a job.

ANTHOLOGIES

The Making of an Anthology

I have worked with Apex Publications since 2009; first as a slush reader and freelance editor, then as an assistant editor. I have edited seven anthologies to date for various companies, with more on the way. When Jason asked me if I wanted to write a regular column for the Apex blog, I was happy to. I knew exactly what I wanted to write about: my process for creating an anthology.

Before I started editing and writing for anthologies, the entire process was a locked door mystery. I had no idea how anthologies were created and why some stories were chosen over others. I wanted to open the door to my particular process and shed some light on the decisions that go into creating an anthology.

I am grateful to Jason and Apex Publications for giving me the opportunity to reveal the mystery that is the making of an anthology. To put the column in context, I asked Jason to talk about Apex Publications and the website that gave my column a home.

Apex Publications by Jason Sizemore

What is Apex Publications?

Apex is a book and magazine publisher of science fiction, fantasy, and horror. Our focus has always been on the weird, the interstitial. Fiction that can be hard to define, and usually causes me fits when I try to explain the type of work we produce; weird genre work with a pinch of literary sensibilities.

We've published anthologies, collections, novellas, and novels, mostly in trade paperback format. However, the company originated back in 2004 with a digest-sized magazine called Apex Science Fiction and Horror Digest. Eventually, the digest grew into a beast, something more than one mortal man could handle, so I ceased publication after a double-sized twelfth issue. By that point, our circulation was 7,500 readers, 800 subscribers, and a print run of 4,500. Because I could not divorce myself from short fiction, Apex Digest was reborn as Apex Magazine in a cheaper to produce digital format.

The digital zine turned me on to eBooks, just in time for the beginning of the digital book revolution. As a professional software developer, I'm intrigued by the possibilities of eBooks, and over the past twelve months, I've been turning the Apex ship more in that direction. My current goal is to leverage Apex along with my software skills to produce memorable and outstanding interactive digital books within the next twelve to eighteen months.

Apex has been an important part of my life for the past seven years. My wife calls Apex my "third child." To that extent, she's partially right. I have a love for the business that drives me to work an insane amount of hours for very little financial recompense. The reward, to me, has always been about producing a fantastic product. Books can change the world, and I like to think that every book I produce changes the world just a fraction.

I believe others share this same view. I have no other explanation for the insane numbers of amazing editors, authors, artists, and graphic designers who pitch in to make Apex a success, most of them volunteers. Whether it's a shared passion to change the world one book at a time, or simple philanthropy, I am eternally grateful for their help. Without these kind individuals, there would be no Apex.

Genre fans are known to be loyal... as long as you treat them well and bring out consistently entertaining product. I do my best to do both. To that end, we have some of the best fans in the business. They're vocal, friendly, and supportive. When I meet our fans at conventions, bookstores, or even online, I quickly come to realize why I'm still doing Apex even after seven long years. Their enthusiasm and praise make all the long hours and frustration worth every minute.

The Making of an Anthology, Part 1: Introduction

As part of the editorial staff of Apex Publications, I've been asked to clear up some of the mystery that surrounds the making of an anthology. I've agreed to do so—from my point of view. I am just one editor. My way is not the One True Way. This is just what works for me and how I approach each project.

This is going to be a nine part feature (including this article). In each part, I will delve into what I do and why I do it that way. I will talk about some of the things anthologists (editors of anthologies) need to think about that may not be obvious on the surface. Here is how I'm going to break it out:

Part 1: Introduction – What I'm doing and how I will break out my topics.

Part 2: Invitations – Who I invite and how I make that decision.

Part 3: Choosing the right stories for an anthology – The read through of all of the stories and why some stories make it while others do not.

Part 4: Acceptance is just the beginning: editorial rounds and contracts – What happens after a story is accepted but before the contract is sent out to the author.

Part 5: Thoughts on the TOC – Putting the stories in the right order for the best overall impact in a cohesive theme.

Part 6: The perfect anthology bio – What I would love to see in an author's bio for an anthology. Too often I get too little, too much, or something that is wholly inappropriate.

Part 7: Proofers – After the full manuscript is done, how to keep the typos and stupid mistakes from breeding.

Part 8: Editorial interns – How I teach the craft of creating an effective anthology to others.

Part 9: After the anthology manuscript is turned into the publisher – Your work is not done after the manuscript is off your desk. The aftercare of an anthology.

There you have it. By the end of this series you will have a good understanding of what goes on behind the scenes during the making of an anthology.

The Making of an Anthology, Part 2: Invitations

The first time I was invited to an invite-only anthology, I was over the moon. I was new enough that I didn't realize that there were such animals. I thought that I just kept missing the calls for submissions. After that, I knew that the anthologies were out there but I didn't know how to get invitations. It took me a while to get the hang of it. Every editor and publishing house is different.

When I became an editor, I discovered how hard it was to be on the other side of the desk. At this point, I limit myself to invitation-only anthologies but I'm a little more lax than some of my counterparts in the industry; especially when it comes to small press anthologies. This is how I determine if I'm going to invite an author to submit to a project.

First Round of Invitations

For the first twenty, I go to my rolodex of authors and pick ones I know I want to work with again. These are authors I have worked with in the past, but not too recently and I know they do good work. After that, I talk with the publisher about their authors and invite around ten of them. I round out the list by inviting ten authors from my second-tier list; authors I haven't published before but I've read their stuff or who come highly recommended to me.

That's forty authors for a small press anthology. I like to send out between forty to fifty invitations. Based on experience, I get about a 60% return. The last ten invitation slots go to my random Facebook and Twitter call. This is how I find new talent. I ask for authors who have had at least one sale. IE: Someone paid the author money for a story and they bought a latte or paid a bill with it. Also, these last ten invitation slots can also be used for new authors I meet at conventions.

That's between forty to fifty author invites per anthology, knowing I'll get about a 60% return and I'll end up publishing about 50%-75% of those authors who respond to the invitation and write me a story.

- 20 invites for 1st tier authors from my rolodex.
- 10 invites for publisher recommended authors.
- 10 invites for 2nd tier authors from my rolodex.
- 10 invites for new talent.

Considerations for Invitations

Let's back up a moment. Some of you might want to know how to get into my rolodex and be considered for my personal 1st and 2nd tier slots. I can tell you upfront that a lot of it is subjective. How you treated me when I met you at a convention before and after you knew who

I was. How professional you were at the meeting (business card, politeness, etc...) How other editors have talked about you. If we worked together in the past, how hard or easy that working relationship was and a myriad of other factors influence my decision.

One big factor is what you write on the internet—especially if I don't know you. If you, as an author, spend a lot of time talking crap about other authors or editors, I'm probably not going to work with you because I don't think you'll be easy to work with. If you spend a lot of time bemoaning your fate at not getting a particular sale, I'm going to wonder what kind of emotional handholding I'm going to need to do with you through the editing process.

True story—I had one author on an invite list for a major publishing house anthology after reading their book for a review. However, their reaction to my review (focusing only on the negative portions of it and ignoring the positive things I had to say) and publicly trashing me on a social networking site, made me remove that author from the invite list. All I could think was: if this is how they reacted to a less-than-stellar review, then how difficult will they be to work with on the upcoming project—especially through the editing phase?

The harder I think you will be to work with, the less likely I will be to invite you to any project.

However, I have also had polite and professional disagreements with authors that have left me respecting them and willing to work with them again. Manners are a good thing and courtesy works.

Pinch Hitter Invitations

Sometimes I've needed to fill holes in the anthology I was working on. I didn't meet my project word count or there were particular things I was looking for that I didn't get. That's when I turn to my Pinch Hitter list.

For me, a Pinch Hitter author is one of my 1st or 2nd tier authors with whom I've worked with before in some capacity, know they can take specific instructions, and can get me a good story in a very short amount of time. This is the kind of author that I can turn to and ask *"How's your schedule for the next 10 days?"* who will answer me truthfully about whether or not they have time. Then, they will answer me honestly when I ask something like, *"Can you get me a 4000 word story based around something that is not human becoming human for a day? Something like an angel or immortal solider?"*

This is the point where they can say "No," because I respect their ability to know what they can and cannot do. Pinch Hitter authors are some of the authors I hold in the highest esteem. A lot of them are not on the original invite list because I used them recently in another project and I like to spread the invitation love around. These are the authors who understand that I'm crafting an overall arcing project that needs a story that fits exactly. They work fast, ask appropriate questions, and earn my undying gratitude.

The Whole Package

There you have it. This is how I decide which authors should be invited to what project. It's not an exact science but it is based on experience, manners, and investigation. I look at my list of people I've worked with before, the quality of work they delivered and whether or not it was on time. I look to publisher, author, and editor recommendations. Finally, I take a chance on new talent—after looking them up to see what they have to say. If all that doesn't pan out, I've got my Pinch Hitters to turn to in a time of need.

The Making of an Anthology, Part 3: Choosing the Right Stories

I have said several times that stories that don't get into my anthologies aren't *bad* stories. They just aren't the *right* stories for the anthology. It occasionally breaks my heart to have to turn away beautifully written and entertaining stories because they just don't fit into the overall project I am creating.

When it comes to choosing stories for an anthology, I look at the following things: Is the story technically correct? How much effort will I have to spend to make the story work for the anthology? Will it fit into the overall arc of the anthology that I want to produce? Some of it is touchy-feely. Some of it comes down to the time and effort I will spend to make the story exactly how I want it.

Technical Proficiency

Even when an author is invited to an anthology, technical proficiency is a must; maybe even more important on invitation-only anthologies. By inviting an author, I have a higher level of expectation for them and their skills than I would for an open call.

When I read for invite-only projects, I read every story all the way through—whether or not I like it at first blush. Obvious spelling and grammar errors are annoying and make me wonder how much time the author put into the story. For most authors, they have had months of warning which warrants at least one pass through with a second set of eyes before I see the story in question. It is a show of professionalism and respect.

Technical mistakes mean more work for me and make me question whether or not the author has the writing chops to do the work that I need. Yes, I understand I am making assumptions. However, I am going off the story I have in front of me and not my understanding of the author's reputation, not my personal friendship with the author, and not what they have sold before. All I care about is the story before me and what I'm going to have to do to get it into shape.

Rewrite Work Needed

Beyond the technical aspect of the story, there is the subject matter and tone to consider. Is the story perfect as is or a mess? If it is a mess, can the story be salvaged for the anthology with a rewrite request? Is there a logical fallacy in the first couple of paragraphs that invalidates the rest of the story that can be fixed with edits? Does only one aspect need to be changed or would the whole story need to be rewritten?

I think about these things because if I don't catch them early, and anything slips through, readers will catch the mistakes, or the tonal shift, and wonder what I was thinking the day I edited the story.

If a story is very close but not quite right, I will ask for edits if I know that the author is willing to accept editorial direction. Not every author is. If the story is too much work to edit to make it fit, it gets rejected. This is why, when invited to an invitation-only or "closed" anthology, you should feel free to ask questions of the editor to make sure you are on the right track.

Overall Arc of the Anthology

This is the hardest part of making an anthology. Each book is different. There is a set theme, genre, and tone for the project. Every single story must fit into the whole of the anthology without one standing out too much. I liken it to a string of pearls. Every pearl must be similar in shape, size, and luster or it stands out in a bad way, breaking the cohesiveness of the necklace.

For *Close Encounters of the Urban Kind* (Apex Publications), I received a number of fabulous stories that I could not use. Some stories did not fit the "encounter" part of the anthology. Some stories did not fit the "urban legend" part of the anthology. And some stories did not fit the dark tone that I was going for. For *Human Tales* (Dark Quest Books), I received a lot of fabulous stories about the exact same cautionary tale and could only accept one of them. I also received some wonderful stories where the supernatural creature won in the end—which went counter to the cautionary theme of dealing with humans.

If the story I'm reading could easily fit with an edit request to any part of the story, I am more likely to take it than a story that needs an entire thread reworked. Again, it comes down to the ease of work involved. I don't want to accept 6 out of 15 stories that need major edits—technical or otherwise.

I work the most with authors who "get it" and with authors who understand how to take editorial direction. In the end, the editor is creating the anthology to their own specification and the editor is the one responsible for the end product. That often means rejecting beautiful stories while accepting stories that still need a little (but not a lot) of work.

The Making of an Anthology, Part 4: Edits - Acceptance is Only the Beginning

Once a story has been accepted, my work really begins. This means I need to do line editing and copy editing. To make sure we are on the same page, here are the definitions that I am working with. *Line editing* is the process in which a manuscript is edited for tone, logic, and consistency. (IE: Making sure there are no plot holes or info dumps, etc...) *Copy editing* is the work that an editor does to improve the formatting, style, and accuracy of text. (IE: Everything is spelled correctly, killing adverbs, removing passive tense, and making sure there are no missing or repeated words, etc...)

Editorial Rounds

For my anthologies, every story goes through at least two editorial rounds before I hand the story back to the author. First, I line edit the story. I make sure that there are bullets in the gun on the mantel, that the hero isn't punching people with a broken hand without the appropriate reaction, and that the historic event in question really did happen when the author stated it happened. This type of editing makes the story stronger and helps keep the suspension of disbelief in the reader.

In the second round, I copy edit the story. I look specifically at the technical aspects of the writing. Is the author fond of mixing verb tenses? Are there spelling mistakes or dropped words? Is the prose infected with the dreaded adverb or too much passive voice? Are there contractions where there shouldn't be contractions? This type of editing allows the prose to be invisible so there are no mistakes to pull the reader out of the story.

Then I hand the story with the line and copy edits back to the author. Sometimes there are rewrite requests. Sometimes there aren't. The author needs to accept or reject my changes. If they reject something, they need to put a comment as to why they are rejecting it.

Rewrite Edits

Usually less intensive, any story that has completed rewrites needs to go through another round of line and copy edits. This is just good due diligence. You never know what new mistake can be introduced when fixing an old mistake. Most new mistakes are based around starting a sentence with one thought in mind and finishing it with another.

Acceptance on Both Sides

Once I have finished my edits and the author has accepted or rejected my edits *and* we have come to an accord over the finished story, then I send out the contract. The main reason for this is the sad fact of life that, sometimes, an editor and an author cannot come to an accord on a story. For whatever reason, the author will not accept the requested changes and the editor will not accept the story without the requested changes.

If a contract had been signed between the editor and author before this point, they would be at an impasse. However, without a signed contract, the author is free to withdraw their story and the editor is free to apologize and reject the story as is.

Note: There is a good way to withdraw your story and there is a bad way. Politeness and courtesy rule the day. The person who said, "I don't like your hackneyed idea of prose" will never be invited back to another project while the person who said, "I'm sorry, I think this story is no longer a good fit for your anthology" will.

Everyone Needs Edits

At the end of the day, every story needs edits—whether it is to make sure it fits the anthology or to correct technical mistakes. For me, I do 1-3 editorial rounds with the author until we both are happy. Then contracts can be sent out and signed in good faith.

Making of an Anthology, Part 5: Thoughts on the Table of Contents

Once I have all of the stories for an anthology bought, edited, and polished, I need to put them in the right order. Up until this point, I have had a basic Table of Contents or "TOC" in mind. Frequently, as I read and say "yes" to a story, I will place it mentally in my line up. Sometimes, this organically grown TOC becomes fact. Most of the time, it does not. There are too many other factors involved in how I put an anthology together.

For me, there are three main things to consider when setting up a TOC for the best overall impact of the anthology's theme: organization, social niceties, and anchor stories.

Organization

What is the overall organization of the anthology? In *Close Encounters of the Urban Kind*, I set up the anthology like the telling of an urban legend with the stories explaining the least in the front with each subsequent story giving more details on how and why they were happening. In other anthologies, I have broken the stories out by genre or I have placed the stories chronologically. In several anthologies, I have subsections. *Beast Within 2* has a "predator" section and a "prey" section. Whatever organization I set up, it is all designed to have each story flow into the next one in an overall cohesive whole.

Social Niceties

What common customs and courtesies should I be aware of? This may seem like a strange thing to be concerned with while putting anthologies together but it plays a part. For example, I usually don't want to start off an anthology with something that has a major phobia in it. Usually.

In *Close Encounters of the Urban Kind*, the first story "Lollo" has a killer alien clown. Coulrophobia is something I am aware of. But, I did not believe that "Lollo" would turn readers off of the anthology. However, in another anthology, despite wanting to put the were-spider story first, I did not because arachnophobia is a far more prevalent phobia and it could turn readers away. Plus, there was sex in that story.

Which brings me to the next social nicety I need to be aware of: sex and the myriad of problems it could bring. While I live in a fairly open and sex positive city, people—like my mother; an avid reader—live below the bible belt and I need to be aware that sex is uncomfortable for some readers. Placing a sex filled story at the beginning of the anthology might give the wrong impression and the anthology an unexpected or unintended reputation.

There are a number of controversial things that pop up in SFF/horror stories that require thought on where to place those stories in an anthology. What you may not consider to be a big deal might be scandalous to another. It is just something to be aware of.

Anchor Stories

What is the first impression you want to give your reader and the last? Anchor stories are very important in anthologies. These are the first two and last two stories in the book. You want to put your strongest, most archetypical stories in the anchor slots. These are the stories that people will read first for their first impression. These are also the stories they will read last that will stick with them the longest. These are also the stories that casual readers will read while browsing, so you want the stories to grab them and hold tight.

Just because a story is not in an anchor position doesn't mean it isn't a great story. I frequently have to fight with myself on which story will get the anchor positions. I never accept a story that I don't love because, by the end, I will have read and reread it 6-10 times. Anchor stories must be strong, must embody exactly what kind of story I want to tell in the anthology, and must fit the organization I set up for that anthology.

When you look at the Table of Contents for an anthology, know that an editor has taken the time to place that story where it is for a reason. There is a lot of behind-the-scenes thinking to putting together the right anthology TOC to create the best overall impact for the reader.

The Making of an Anthology, Part 6: The Perfect Anthology Biography

Every one of my anthologies has a biographies section or the author's biography attached to their story. A good biography tells you something interesting about the author: if they've been published before, if they have won any awards, and where a reader can look to find out more about the author. Sometimes, the biography will also tell the reader about the story written for the anthology.

When it comes to biographies written for anthologies I edit, I prefer simple and professional biographies, usually of about 200 words in length.

Some Things to Remember

Text is an imperfect medium for expressing emotion. Humor and sarcasm often fall flat and make the author seem uneducated or arrogant.

Your biography is not the time for you to put yourself down. "This is my first published story and I'm thankful the editor didn't toss it in the trash," is not a good biography statement. Just stick with the facts. "*The Mighty Crow* is Jennifer's first published story," is simple and direct.

Unless your nickname is the name you write under, don't include it in your biography unless it is something the editor requests. Jennifer

"Apocalypse Girl" Brozek does not belong in the bio of my *Westward Weird* anthology story while it is perfect in the bio of my *No Man's Land* military sci-fi story because all of the authors have a call sign included in their biography.

Your Biography is Your Calling Card

You want your biography to be generic enough to give the reader information about you as an author and keep your most current sales upfront. Think about the information on your business card: Who are you? What do you do and what are you known for? How can someone get in touch with you? Tell us something more about you.

Who are you?
- Jennifer is an award winning editor, author and game designer.
- Jennifer is the editor of seven anthologies including the award winning GRANTS PASS anthology.
- Jennifer is a freelance author for numerous RPG companies.

What do you do and what are you known for?
- Winner of the 2009 Australian Shadows Award for best edited publication, Jennifer has edited seven anthologies with more on the way.
- Author of *In a Gilded Light* and *The Little Finance Book That Could*, Jennifer has more than forty-five published short

stories, and is an assistant editor for the award winning Apex Publications.

- Winner of both the Origins and the ENnie award, Jennifer's contributions to RPG sourcebooks include *Dragonlance*, *Colonial Gothic*, *Shadowrun*, *Serenity*, *Savage Worlds*, and White Wolf SAS.

How can someone get in touch with you?

- When she is not writing her heart out, she is gallivanting around the Pacific Northwest in its wonderfully mercurial weather.
- Jennifer is an active member of SFWA and HWA.
- Read more about her at her blog: http://www.jenniferbrozek.com/blog/

The Long and Short of It

To be honest, I hate writing my biography. Thus, I spend the time upfront to write out biographies of different lengths (50, 150, 300 words). I update these biographies on a regular basis to reflect new sales I've made and awards I've won. I have a couple of short biographies featuring my writing or my editing and one long biography that covers it all. This way, I don't have to worry about scrambling to write something when an editor asks me for an up-to-date bio.

This is what I want my authors to do: provide me with a straightforward, professional, current biography that sticks to the facts and allows the reader to find out more about them. The well prepared biography can go a long way for the author.

The Making of an Anthology, Part 7: The Value of Proofers

Proofread: *To check a written text for errors in spelling and grammar, to find errors and mark correction.*

When it comes to proofreading, I have two levels of proofing for my anthologies. The first happens before the final manuscript goes to the publisher. The second happens after the final manuscript comes back from the publisher.

Pre-Publisher Proof

By the time I have a final manuscript with the table of contents, biography section, and all of the stories in order, I have read every story at least four times: upon receipt, edit round, polish round, and TOC line up consideration. Four times is enough to make me too familiar with the story to find every single mistake. That is why I bring in outside eyes in the form of trusted proofers.

I have between one to three proofers per anthology. I break up the stories by section and parcel out the tasks. My proofers know they are the last line of defense between the reader and that last damnable typo. These typos included dropped words, substituted words ('right' instead of 'write') and dropped/added letters ('be' instead of 'been', 'not' instead of 'no').

Occasionally, one of my proofers will find a glaring mistake—like a character being unable to smell in the first paragraph and subsequent statements of said character smelling something later—and for that, I am immensely grateful. However, most of the time, my proofers catch those tiny mistakes—*I swear they breed like gremlins!*—that readers may or may not catch that I will invariably see once it is too late.

Post-Publisher Proof

Once the publisher has received the final manuscript, they typeset it and return it to the editor for a final look. This version of the proof is called a "galley" or "advance reader's copy" or ARC. This kind of proofing is the most important and the most minimal proofing you can get away with. It is also the time to look for the formatting errors introduced by the software used to do the typesetting. Added and dropped italics are one of the most prevalent problems.

If I have an opportunity, I send this ARC out to the anthology authors and ask them to proof their own story. Sixteen to twenty pairs of fresh eyes with a vested interest in the look and feel of their story is the best way to find those last couple of hidden typos. Every author and editor knows this is it: Find the mistake or forever hold your peace.

Mistakes Do Happen

The most vexing thing of all is that no matter how many times you look, or how many proofers have been added to the mix, mistakes get through. Don't kill yourself over it. When the emails come in nitpicking a typo, all you can do is either not respond or thank the reader for their diligence.

Typos will make you crazy. But once the anthology is out the door, the best thing you can do as an author or editor is to keep your crazy on the inside. Most people won't notice the typo. Or, they will and then move on. Of course, beforehand, you and your proofers will do their best to slay those breeding beasts.

The Making of an Anthology, Part 8: Editorial Interns

Frequently, as part of the creation of an anthology, I choose one person who has expressed interest in learning how to put together an anthology to be my editorial intern. This person learns the business side of anthologies as well as other nuances of the publishing industry. Most of my interns have gone on to put together their own successful anthologies.

There are a number of things I have my editorial interns do to teach them the way I work. This includes them being CC'd on all email, producing a single manuscript from edits, collecting all those nitpicky details editors need to have, and the all important "other duties as assigned."

Copied on All Email

There are two main reasons that my interns are CC'd on all email between me and the author. First, the intern needs to see how I communicate with the author. This communication spans everything from general information dispersal to answering queries to discussions of edits to final manuscript preparation. Second, the authors will eventually be communicating directly with my intern while CC'ing me.

Some say there is an art to email between editor and author. I say it is business—friendly and personal—but business nonetheless. Thus, when it comes to editorial disagreements, it is important that my intern understand how to handle such in a professional manner. No matter how emotional, upset, or angry I may be about something, it is important that all communications between author and editor be simple, factual, and professional.

Also, there is a time to push back on editorial disagreements and a time to let things go. Being CC'd on all email gives my intern a real world backseat view into this. Thus, when it is their turn to contact the authors for whatever I need, they have already seen how I handle them and my intern can act accordingly.

Collecting Edits into a Single Manuscript

The biggest job of an editor is to edit. Thus, after my first round of edits, I have my intern collect all of the author responses to those edits. The intern compiles all of the completed stories into a single manuscript while informing me of any stories that either did not accept edits or, in their opinion, need more edits. At that point, I look at the story, discuss the issues with them and then proceed as needed— going back to the author or accepting the pushback.

Having my intern collect the edited stories into a single manuscript gives them a chance to see how pieces and parts become a cohesive whole. It is at this point that my intern can suggest other possible needed edits and/or a change in the lineup of the table of contents. They return to me a manuscript that is ready for my polish.

Gathering Details

When it comes to putting together anthologies, the devil is in the details... and there are a lot of details to get. This is a task I give my intern so that when they eventually do their own anthology, they know upfront what kinds of details are needed. These details can include (but aren't limited to): Full names, postal addresses, email addresses, Paypal email addresses, phone numbers, biographies, preferred method of payment, and social security number.

A subset of this information needs to be packaged up and sent to the publisher while another set of information is used in the anthology. Still a third subset is kept on file for when you need to contact the author, set up readings in their area, or manage something for the publisher.

Other Duties as Assigned

Finally, there is the all important 'other duties as assigned." This really could be anything. Accompany me to a convention or a reading where the anthology is highlighted. Write a press release for the publisher's website.

Distribute information to the authors on release date, payment date, where the comp copies are, and find out who hasn't be paid or hasn't received their book yet.

This section, other duties as assigned, teaches my intern that even when the final manuscript has been turned in, the job is not done. There is a host of other duties to attend to. These duties are nebulous and teachable only through experience.

The Making of an Anthology, Part 9: After the Anthology Manuscript is Turned In

This is the final article in the *Making of an Anthology* series. This article details some of the jobs the editor needs to do after the final manuscript has been turned in and the anthology is on its way to being released. These jobs include author aftercare, PR and marketing, anthology events, and reviews.

Aftercare of the Authors

As an editor, the authors of my anthology are "my" authors and I want to do right by them. I want to make sure they have been paid as well as received all of the books in their contract. I also want them to know when the book comes out and if we get any really good reviews. I work to take care of my authors after the anthology is done because I will probably work with them again and they will be a part of the anthologies' success. I want them to be as excited as I am.

PR & Marketing

Some of the success of an anthology comes from getting the anthology out there in front of eyes to see, buy, and read it. That takes marketing effort in the form of press releases, ads in the appropriate places, and the judicious use of social networking. Putting the information out there is good. A constant barrage of "buy this anthology" is not.

That's where PR comes in. This comes in the form of interviews, contests, and other things that work with the reputations of those involved and not just around the fact that there is a new product out there. It is important to bring the human (author) element into things. Being a real person and interesting will often get a book bought as quickly as a well placed advertisement. It is part of the editor's job to help the authors do that.

Events: Readings and Conventions

This all leads to events that showcase the anthology in question: readings and conventions. I've discovered that having more than one author at an event will often bring in more of an audience; the more people there are, the more excitement generated at the event, about the book, and about the host location. As an editor, I'm there to lend moral support, attend to details, introduce the authors, and cheer everyone on. The anthology is my project and the authors are a part of that.

Thus, it lands on me to either set up the readings, encourage them, or to help the authors in whatever way I can. This is part aftercare and part marketing/PR. It all links together.

Reviews

Finally, once the book is out there, it falls to the readers to judge your anthology. For good or ill, it is in the readers hands and all you can do at this point is to hope for the best and learn from the critiques. I tend to avoid reviews unless they are specifically pointed out to me by friends, my authors, or my publisher. Then I read with as open a mind as possible.

Obviously, good reviews are great. But, bad reviews happen. After all that work, some may not care for the book. At that point, all you can do is accept it and move on. If I have time, I'll forward the more interesting reviews to my authors. Reviews—good and bad—are like responses to a story submittal: they are proof that you are out there, doing what you set out to do.

How to Create an Effective Anthology Proposal

From the moment I published my first anthology, *Grants Pass*, I have been asked "How did you do it?" This question is not as simple as it sounds. What is actually being asked is a series of questions: What did you do to get your anthology accepted? Who did you know? How did you pitch the anthology to the publisher? How can I learn to do what you did?

I call the *Grants Pass* anthology "the little anthology that could" because it took me five years to get it published. It was a great concept and I was not willing to give it up. I received twenty-one rejections before the anthology was accepted. Even then, half of the already accepted stories had to be booted from the manuscript.

During the first part of those five years, I was flying blind and learning as I went along. Over time, I taught myself this basic outline on how to do a one-page anthology pitch to different publishing houses—small and large—as well as how and when to approach publishing houses with the pitch. With seven anthologies in three years, I must be doing something right.

The Nuts and Bolts of the One Page Anthology Pitch

When it comes to anthology pitches, you need to give the publishers all of the information they need up front. This is the basic information that I give: Title, Editor(s), Total Word Count, Logline, Concept, Proposal, Authors Attached (Optional), and the Budget (Optional).

Having this information gives both you and the publisher a good understanding of what the anthology is and where you want to go. It is an excellent way of putting both of you on the same page for the project. It also gives the publishers the pertinent details to create a contract.

Digging into the Details

Let's dig deeper into this information that you should provide to the publishing house.

Title: The title of any anthology is a first impression and a promise to the reader on what it is about. Think about the anthology you want to create and choose appropriately. Once introduced, the publisher can keep this title in mind while reading the rest of the proposal.

Editor: Putting this information up front lets the publisher know who is doing the work. It also helps with name recognition if you have a more famous co-editor working with you.

Word Count: Most anthologies run between 70,000 and 125,000 words. Some go much longer. They are rarely shorter. This will give the publisher a size of the book they will be working with. It also gives the editor a base line for how many authors they need. An 80,000 word anthology need about 20 authors writing an average of 4000 words each. Something to consider when thinking about budgets and authors.

Logline: The first time I saw the term "logline" I had to ask what it meant. Primarily used in screen writing, it is a one or two line sentence answering the question: What is this all about? When I answer the question, I include genre and market in my answer: A sci-fi themed anthology about colony ships. A YA horror anthology about getting lost in corn mazes. The logline puts the publisher in the correct frame of mind.

Concept: The concept is the flavor text of the proposal. Think of it like the descriptive blurb on the back of a book. This is where the editor can write in-character to make the pitch interesting and give the tone of the anthology. Setting the tone is in the phrases and words that you use.

Proposal: The proposal is the business end of the pitch. This is where you state the professional level of the anthology (semi-pro, pro), how many authors you intend to have in the anthology, the non-fiction explanation of the concept previously alluded to, and anything else you believe the publisher should know. IE: Historically accurate basis, shared world anthology, or all former military authors.

Authors Attached: This is an optional section of the anthology pitch. If you have contacted authors who have already agreed to be in the anthology, you may put those names here. The bigger the name, the more likely the interest. However, be careful. If you sell an anthology based around a single big named author who then backs out (for whatever reason) it could spell all kinds of trouble.

In the real world example of an anthology proposal below, after I pitched the anthology, the publishing house came back and asked for a list of possible authors. I then emailed a sample list of authors I have a good working relationship with and stated that the authors were possible based on schedule and payment but I did not promise any one of them to the anthology. Then, I invited the publishing house to send me a wish list of authors and I would see if I could get in contact with them.

Budget: This is another optional section of your proposal where you budget out the upfront costs of the anthology. This does not include royalties.

Based on the professional level of the anthology, you can determine how much an anthology is going to cost. With an 80,000 word anthology, the numbers break out like this. Flat fee of $20/story = $400. Flat fee of $50/story = $1000. Semi-pro rate of $0.01/word = $800. Pro-rates start at a minimum of $0.05/word = $4,000. And that is just for the authors. You need to determine your own editorial fee as well.

While most publishing houses have their own artists, I often bring outside artists into the publishing house for the covers to my anthologies. This is rare. But if you can offer it with a specific rate, it does not hurt to include that into your budget.

Real World Example
Below is a real world example of an anthology pitch I sent out to a small press that accepted my proposal.

Title: *Coins of Chaos*

Editor: Jennifer Brozek

Word Count: 70,000 – 80,000

Logline: Horror anthology based around depression era art called Hobo Nickels. Wikipedia entry on hobo nickels - http://en.wikipedia.org/wiki/Hobo_nickel and inspiration for the anthology - http://www.thisiscolossal.com/2011/09/skull-nickels/

Concept: Miniature works of art or pieces of magic, hobo nickels fascinate, delight, and terrify. In the *Coins of Chaos*, sixteen coins carry a curse of death, destruction, and ill luck. Sent into the world by the Carver, these sixteen coins have fed his evil design since 1913, ruining countless lives. These are some of those stories. Had a run of bad luck lately? Check your pockets and make sure you haven't picked up one of these cursed coins on accident.

Proposal: I am putting together a semi-pro level invitation only anthology of sixteen horror stories from 1913 to present day that focus on one of these hobo nickels as a catalyst for that which will befall the protagonists of the story. The coin itself does not cause the pain, but once the coin enters the lives of the protagonists, it all goes wrong.

Budget: The upfront cost of this anthology to the publishing house is $X,XXX - $X,XXX. This is to be paid upon acceptance of the completed manuscript to Jennifer Brozek who will then distribute the money to the authors and cover artist.

I intend to pay a flat fee of $XX per story ($XXX). My editorial fee is $XXX. If your publishing house does not have an in-house artist, I know a number of artists and photographers who can do cover art at $XXX for the piece including Shane Tyree, Alina Pete and Amber Clark.

When, Who, and How to Pitch

Once you have honed your anthology pitch to a concisely worded single page, it is time to pitch. Pitching anthologies is a bit different than pitching novels. You are not trying to sell a completed product. You are selling a concept of a product that will have many authors.

For the most part, there are no "open calls" for anthologies. Thus, when to pitch is a delicate balance of timing and luck. When at an event where networking is possible, asking if a publisher is open to anthology queries will tell you whether or not you can get your foot in the door. You can have a hard copy of the pitch with you but do not offer it to the publisher unless they ask. If they are open to the concept, more often than not, they will tell you email the proposal to them.

When you are not at an event, the best you can do is look through the publishers you believe are right for your anthology based on company history and genre and then email the query, asking if they accept anthology proposals. Sometimes you get lucky.

As for who you really want to contact—that would be the acquisitions manager/editor of the publishing house. You may have to climb through the ranks of various lower rung publishing house employees to do it. Don't be afraid to ask who the right person is in a particular publishing house.

Which brings me to my final thought on pitching anthologies. Always be professional. It does not matter who you are attempting to pitch to or ask information of, publishing is a business. If you cannot be polite, courteous, and professional to everyone you meet, you won't go far. Publishing is a small business and industry professionals talk to each other.

Recommended Reading

Conventions for the Aspiring Game Professional
by Jess Hartley

Elements of Style by Strunk & White

The 10% Solution by Ken Rand

Terrible Minds Blog - http://terribleminds.com/

Matt Forbeck's Blog -
http://www.forbeck.com/

Jennifer Brozek's Blog -
http://www.jenniferbrozek.com/blog/

Ryan Macklin's Blog -
http://ryanmacklin.com/

About the Author

Jennifer Brozek is an award winning editor and author.

Winner of the 2009 Australian Shadows Award for best edited publication, Jennifer has edited seven anthologies with more on the way. Author of *In a Gilded Light* and *The Lady of Seeking in the City of Waiting*, she has more than forty-five published short stories.

Jennifer also is a freelance author for numerous RPG companies. Winner of both the Origins and the ENnie award, her contributions to RPG sourcebooks include *Dragonlance*, *Colonial Gothic*, *Shadowrun*, *Serenity*, *Savage Worlds*, and White Wolf SAS.

When she is not writing her heart out, she is gallivanting around the Pacific Northwest in its wonderfully mercurial weather. Jennifer is an active member of SFWA and HWA. Read more about her at her blog:
http://www.jenniferbrozek.com/blog/